Working Dogs

Therapy Dogs

by Kimberly M. Hutmacher

Consulting Editor: Gail Saunders-Smith, PhD

Consultant: Linda Murray, evaluator
Therapy Dogs International

CAPSTONE PRESS
a capstone imprint

Pebble Plus is published by Capstone Press,
151 Good Counsel Drive, P.O. Box 669, Mankato, Minnesota 56002.
www.capstonepub.com

032010
005740CGF10

 Books published by Capstone Press are manufactured with paper
containing at least 10 percent post-consumer waste.

Library of Congress Cataloging-in-Publication Data
Hutmacher, Kimberly.
  Therapy dogs / by Kimberly M. Hutmacher.
    p. cm.—(Pebble plus. Working dogs)
  Includes bibliographical references and index.
  Summary: "Simple text and full-color photos illustrate the traits, training, and duties of therapy dogs"—Provided by
publisher.
  ISBN 978-1-4296-4475-4 (library binding)
  1. Dogs—Therapeutic use—Juvenile literature. 2. Working dogs—Juvenile literature. I. Title. II. Series.
  RM931.D63H88 2011
  615.5—dc22   2009051418

Editorial Credits
Erika Shores, editor; Bobbie Nuytten, designer; Marcie Spence, media researcher; Eric Manske, production specialist

Photo Credits
AP Images/Casa Grande Dispatch, Alan Levine, 17; Independence Daily Reporter, Nick Wright, 21
Capstone Studio/Karon Dubke, cover (collar), 19
Getty Images Inc./Chris Jackson, cover, 1
Landov LLC/Boston Globe/Bill Polo, 5
Newscom, 13, 15; Dave Williams/Wichita Eagle, 11; Eliza Gutierrez, 9
Super Stock Inc., 7

Note to Parents and Teachers

The Working Dogs series supports national social studies standards related to people, places,
and culture. This book describes and illustrates therapy dogs. The images support early readers
in understanding the text. The repetition of words and phrases helps early readers learn new
words. This book also introduces early readers to subject-specific vocabulary words, which are
defined in the Glossary section. Early readers may need assistance to read some words and to
use the Table of Contents, Glossary, Read More, Internet Sites, and Index sections of the book.

Table of Contents

A Helping Paw

Did you know that

some dogs have jobs?

Therapy dogs work

in nursing homes, hospitals,

schools, and libraries.

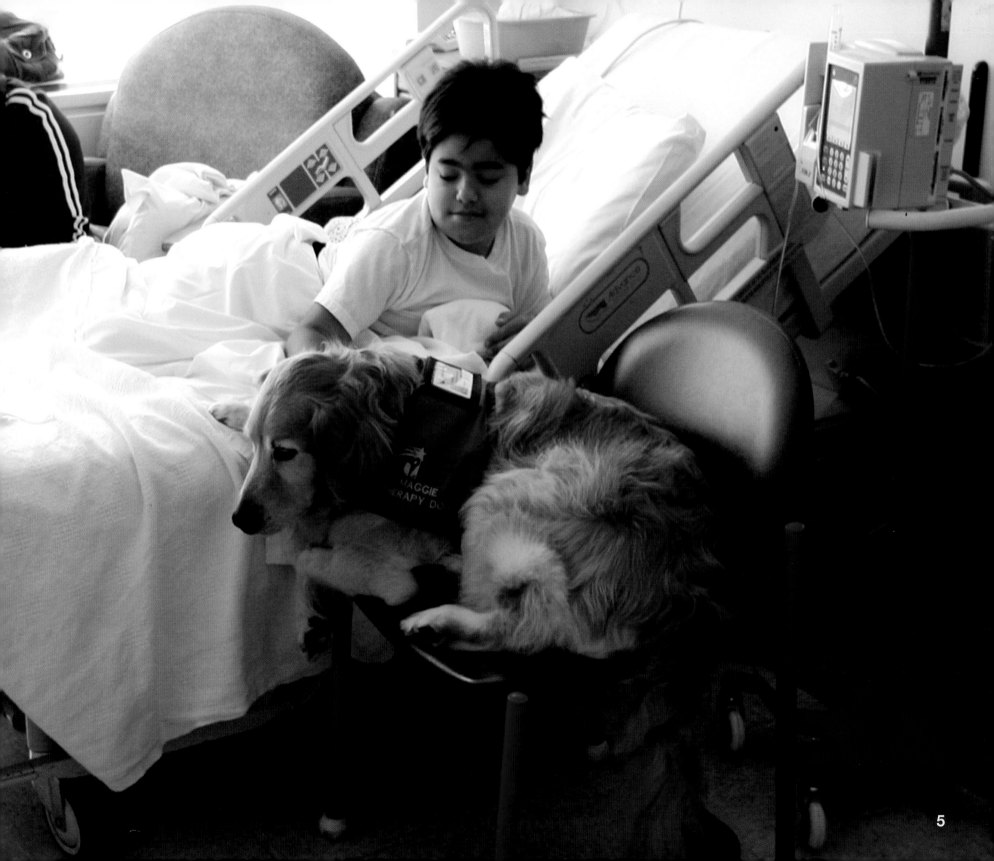

Therapy dogs are friends
to people in need.
People in hospitals feel better
by petting dogs. Elderly people
feel less lonely when dogs visit.

Children practice reading
to therapy dogs.
They think it's more fun
to read to dogs than to adults.

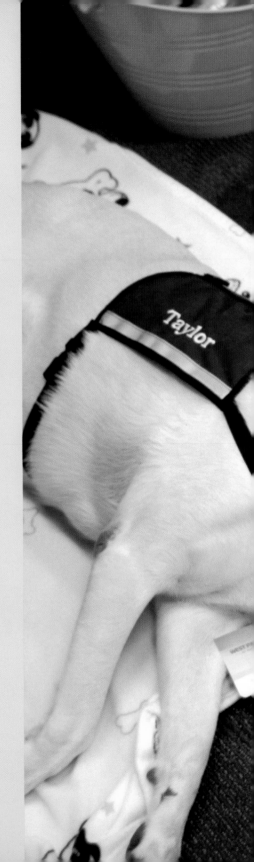

The Right Kind of Dog

All sizes and breeds can be therapy dogs. The dogs must think and act a certain way. The way animals act is called their temperament.

A therapy dog's temperament
is friendly, calm, and smart.
The dogs are good around
new people, animals, and places.

Becoming a Therapy Dog

Some owners train therapy dogs.

Other dogs go to classes.

Dogs learn to always

obey commands such as

"sit" and "stay."

Hospitals have loud machines.
During training, dogs hear
these machines and
other sounds. They learn
not to be scared or bark.

Dogs are tested before becoming therapy dogs. They must walk wearing a loose leash. It proves they follow commands.

Dogs meet new people
and dogs during testing.
If they stay calm and obey,
they pass. Therapy dogs
are ready to go to work.

Glossary

breed—a group of animals that come from common relatives

command—an order to follow a direction

leash—a strap used to hold and control an animal

obey—to follow an order or command

therapy—a treatment for an illness, an injury, or a disability

Read More

Barnes, Julia. *Dogs at Work.* Animals at Work. Milwaukee: Gareth Stevens, 2006.

Tagliaferro, Linda. *Therapy Dogs.* Dog Heroes. New York: Bearport, 2005.

Internet Sites

FactHound offers a safe, fun way to find Internet sites related to this book. All of the sites on FactHound have been researched by our staff.

Here's all you do:

Visit *www.facthound.com*

FactHound will fetch the best sites for you!

Index

Word Count: 189
Grade: 1
Early-Intervention Level: 18